LONDON

LIFE IN THE POST-WAR YEARS

LONDON

LIFE IN THE POST-WAR YEARS

THE PHOTOGRAPHS OF DOUGLAS WHITWORTH

The
History
Press

Above: The equestrian statue of Queen Elizabeth II erected over the main entrance to Selfridge's store in Oxford Street in 1953. In the background is a portrait of the first Queen Elizabeth and the shop's windows displayed scenes of Britain's history from Roman times to the twentieth century.

Frontispiece: Derby County supporters survey the blitzed areas around St Paul's Cathedral on 27 April 1946. From early in the morning, football fans had poured into London for the cup final between Derby County and Charlton Athletic, the first one since the war. Derby County won the match.

Front cover illustration: A wet day on the Strand in 1948.

ACKNOWLEDGEMENTS

I would like to thank the following for their much-valued help:
    B.T. Archives; Pam Carter, The Savoy Hotel; Martine de Geus, The Dorchester Hotel; Clive Hardy; The Honourable Company of Master Mariners; Diane Moxon, The London Hilton Hotel; James Minter, Adam House; Don Press; John Stephenson, James Lock & Co. Ltd; David Tucker, The RED Consultancy.
    I also wish to thank my wife Margaret, for her expertise and invaluable assistance. I dedicate this book to her.

ABOUT THE AUTHOR

Douglas Whitworth has had a lifelong interest in photography which extends beyond his own work to the collection and archiving of early photographs. He lives in Nottingham and has accumulated a large number of old images of the city which he has used with effect in a series of books produced on the history of the area.

First published 2002, this edition 2014

The History Press
The Mill, Brimscombe Port
Stroud, Gloucestershire, GL5 2QG
www.thehistorypress.co.uk

© Douglas Whitworth, 2002, 2003, 2014

The right of Douglas Whitworth to be identified as the Author of this work has been asserted in accordance with the Copyright, Designs and Patents Act 1988.

British Library Cataloguing in Publication Data.
A catalogue record for this book is available from the British Library.

ISBN 978 0 7524 9982 6

Typesetting and origination by The History Press
Printed in India

INTRODUCTION

The London of fifty years ago, when the majority of these photographs were taken, was a city without skyscrapers and St Paul's Cathedral was the tallest building in the capital. London was a magnet for the rest of Britain and the world, and these images are the result of the many weeks I spent there in the late 1940s and early 1950s.

Londoners, in the years immediately after the end of the Second World War, were still in shock from the horrors and hardships of that conflict. During the war there had been a comradeship between all classes of society which had made the suffering more bearable. In the aftermath of the war, Britain endured a continuing austerity that seemed even more severe than during the war years. At the same time, there was optimism in the air as the nation got down to the task of rebuilding a new Britain.

St Paul's Cathedral miraculously escaped major damage during the wartime air raids but the area surrounding the cathedral was almost entirely devastated and for over a decade unrestricted views of St Paul's from the south and the east were possible. Plans for the reconstruction of the City were drawn up with the cathedral as its centrepiece with triumphal steps leading down to the river, plus a limit to the height of buildings in its vicinity. In the event developers were allowed a free-for-all and the way became clear for the haphazard building of office blocks all around it.

Nearly all the City's churches were bombed during the war and although from a distance some appeared undamaged, many remained shells for a number of years before restoration began. Only five churches were completely demolished but there are several cases where only the tower of a church remains.

At first sight Fleet Street too appeared to have escaped major damage in the Blitz, but often only the façades of buildings remained – the rear of the *Daily Telegraph* office was burnt out and St Bride's was completely gutted. The 1940s were still the golden age of Fleet Street, when almost all the offices in the street had some connection with newspapers and the printing trade. Famous pubs such as the Cock Tavern, the Punch and the Old Bell were the haunts of journalists – the Old Cheshire Cheese, with its associations with both Johnson and Goldsmith, generally attracted the tourists.

The Port of London in the 1950s was still the busiest in the world with cranes lining both banks of the River Thames. Specta-

tors would line London Bridge to watch the unloading and loading of cargo boats berthed in the Pool. A sail in a launch from Charing Cross Pier to either Woolwich or Greenwich gave a good impression of the scale of London's docks and of its shipping capacity. This was all to change with the loss of trade with the new independent members of the Commonwealth and the transfer of trade to the containerised ports of Tilbury and Felixstowe. By 1981, with the closure of the Royal group of docks, the Port of London was finally closed.

Until 1956 when the Clean Air Act was passed by Parliament, London was notorious for its 'pea-soup' fogs romanticised in the Sherlock Holmes stories, but a serious health hazard – 4,000 premature deaths were attributed to the great smog of December 1952 which lasted for several days.

In contrast, the summers were then generally sunnier and hotter – the 1947 summer particularly remains in the memory of those who experienced it. It became known as the 'Compton and Edrich Summer' after the Middlesex batsmen of contrasting styles who each scored more runs in that vintage summer than any other cricketer before or since.

Central London in those early post-war years still possessed four major food markets – Smithfield, Leadenhall, Billingsgate and Covent Garden, of which only Smithfield remains. Streets near the markets were a hive of activity throughout the night, with convoys of lorries bringing in deliveries and later with trucks collecting food for the shops and hotels of the metropolis. Every night the narrow streets near Fleet Street were equally busy with newspaper vans racing to the railway stations. By early morning the streets near the markets and newspaper offices were empty apart from street cleaners and workmen patronising the public houses with early morning licensing hours.

Tourists, particularly from America, were beginning to arrive in London in greater numbers, making a contribution to Britain's dollar balance of payments. Luxury goods in London's shops were mainly for export – Britons were still under the yoke of many wartime controls – clothes rationing was in force and food rationing was not to end until 1954.

Londoners were accustomed to seeing US servicemen and women on the streets, but in the late 1940s another American invasion took place in the form of transatlantic culture. Milk bars were replaced by self-service cafés and Wimpy bars – the latter serving hamburgers and hot dogs. These glossy establishments were lit by fluorescent tubes, emitting a brilliant new light. Two American musicals took London by storm in those years; these brash shows, *Oklahoma!* and *Annie Get Your Gun*, were a dramatic departure from the romantic Ivor Novello productions and C.B. Cochran revues that preceded them. Meanwhile, at the London Palladium, American stars such as Danny Kaye, Frank Sinatra, Allan Jones and the Andrews Sisters were playing to capacity houses. Danny Kaye, sitting at the edge of the stage, had his audience captivated.

Cinema-going was then at its peak with innumerable cinemas throughout London. In the West End these were centred on Leicester Square where the major film companies had their showcase theatres. Film premières were important events with Hollywood stars making personal appearances. This was the heyday of British films too; popular stars such as John Mills, Dirk Bogarde, Margaret Lockwood and Anna Neagle were also to be seen attending premières in the West End.

Another free entertainment in London was Petticoat Lane Market held on Sunday mornings in Middlesex Street and the neighbouring streets. Besides being wonderfully entertaining, the market was of great value to the East Enders who for years had been deprived of basic and luxury items. The market is still held today and attracts big crowds who are now mainly tourists.

In 1948, the Olympic Games were held in London. These were the first games to be held after the Second World War – no other major world city had offered to stage them. The track and field events were held in Wembley Stadium and other sports such as football, which was an amateur event, were held at other London venues. The games were a great success and the outstanding athlete was Fanny Blankers-Koen, a Dutch runner who was voted the greatest woman athlete of the twentieth century. These were the first Olympic Games to be covered by television and although only a few hundred sets were then in private use, London department stores showed the events free to eager audiences who crowded round the small television receivers.

The Festival of Britain, held in 1951, was conceived as a celebration of recovery from the war and to mark the centenary of the Great Exhibition of 1851. The Festival, although centred in London, gave the country as a whole a chance to forget the war and to enjoy the entertainments. Unfortunately, the weather in the summer of 1951 was poor, but this did not prevent millions of people flocking to the South Bank Exhibition to see the exhibits and events. A lasting benefit of the Festival was the clearing away of the old buildings between the County Hall and Waterloo Bridge, and the building of the Royal Festival Hall, the first new concert hall to be built in the capital after the war.

In 1953, the Coronation of Queen Elizabeth II captured the imagination of the British people and was heralded as the dawn of a new Elizabethan Age. The capital was splendidly decorated throughout the summer and as Coronation Day approached it became almost impossible to obtain a hotel room in London. A wave of euphoria and optimism swept across the country in the weeks prior to the Coronation. The excitement was increased with the news that a British expedition had climbed Mount Everest – the highest mountain in the world. The Coronation procession through London was watched by nearly three million people lining the route and many millions more watching television for the first time. Only the weather marred the event – after many fine days, Coronation Day was wet and one of the coldest June days of the century.

In the 1950s London began the huge task of reconstruction; temporary buildings were demolished and the bomb-site car parks were disappearing. In the City a rash of tower blocks were erected but the plan for the Barbican Centre was not to be completed until 1982. The Piccadilly Circus saga has lasted even longer and all proposed schemes have been abandoned, leaving the hub of the capital almost unaltered.

In Mayfair, great town houses of the aristocracy demolished in the inter-war years were replaced by American-style hotels and this trend was to continue after the war, particularly on Park Lane and Piccadilly. In the 1940s and 1950s there was still a grandeur in the streets off Piccadilly with many elegant Georgian houses situated in quiet backwaters.

For all the internationalisation of the capital – the skyscrapers, new motorway systems and subways – London remains a unique city with a great deal to offer. The royal parks are a delight, the views from the Thames' bridges are varied and magical, the great buildings unsurpassed and the vitality and resilience of its citizens is unquestioned.

Douglas Whitworth
March 2014

St Paul's Cathedral from Fleet Street in 1948. The view up Ludgate Hill was spoilt by the nineteenth-century railway viaduct then spanning the road, but beyond is the slender spire of St Martin Ludgate contrasting with the great dome of St Paul's. Fleet Street was still the street of newspapers – almost all the London and provincial publications had offices here. Intermingled with the great newspaper offices were innumerable cafés and bars, frequented by journalists and printers. Bars such as Yates's, Mooney's and El Vino had their regular patrons who rarely strayed from them – tourists tended to frequent Lyons' or ABC cafés.

Newspaper offices in Fleet Street, 1949. The great twentieth-century offices of the *Daily Telegraph* and the *Daily Express* stand out from the older buildings, mainly occupied by the provincial newspapers and agencies. On the left, down Wine Office Court is the Old Cheshire Cheese dating from 1667, a haunt of Dr Samuel Johnson. Adjoining it is the Queen of Scots House built in 1905 with a statue of Mary Stuart in an alcove on the front, with next to it, the King and Keys – a public house favoured by the journalists of the *Daily Telegraph*. When the newspaper publishers moved to the docklands and elsewhere in the 1980s, Fleet Street lost much of its character.

Visitors admire the portico of the Mansion House in 1951. This is the official residence of the City of London's Lord Mayor, where banquets and functions are held. Across the Poultry is the pre-war Midland Bank headquarters building, designed by Sir Edwin Lutyens and rightly described as a masterpiece, now unfortunately demolished. The street name is a reminder of the days when food markets were held here from the Middle Ages.

Opposite: The view towards London's river and Westminster from the Stone Gallery of St Paul's Cathedral in 1953. Hemmed in by the huddle of warehouses and offices is the square tower of St Andrew-by-the-Wardrobe, gutted during the Second World War but later restored. By the river is the huge curved frontage of Unilever House built in 1930-1932 on the site of the Royal Hotel. Beyond the River Thames is the waterfront of Southwark and, in the distance, the towers of Westminster.

Ludgate Hill from St Paul's in 1948. The slender spire on the right of the street is St Martin Ludgate, the City church that suffered the least damage of any during the war. At the bottom of the hill, the tallest of all Sir Christopher Wren's churches is St Bride's, apparently unscathed but in fact only a shell. This, one of the loveliest of all Wren churches, was restored in 1957. The north tower of St Paul's on the right was originally intended to have a clock similar to the one in the south tower, but it was never installed.

The Bank of England (on the left) in 1951. The windowless (for security) ground floor was designed by Sir John Soane in 1833 – the massive block rising above was the work of Sir Herbert Baker in the 1920s. The figure of the 'Old Lady of Threadneedle Street' appears in the pediment. On the right, behind the equestrian statue of the Duke of Wellington is the Royal Exchange, although no exchange business is now transacted there. With the nearby Mansion House, these two buildings remain relics of an age which preferred classical porticos and are now dwarfed by the City's tower blocks. In an air raid on 12 January 1941, Bank Station, under this intersection, took a direct hit with great loss of life and creating a huge crater in the road.

Queen Victoria Street and the River Thames from St Paul's in 1948. The Wren church of St Nicholas Cole Abbey on the left, burnt out and missing its spire, has since been restored and is now used by the Free Church of Scotland. Beyond in Upper Thames Street is the tower of St Mary Somerset which was saved from destruction in 1869 when the rest of the church was pulled down. The Blitz of the Second World War gave the authorities the same opportunity to replan the city as had been given to the architects of the seventeenth century after the Great Fire of London. In the event, none of the proposed reconstruction plans were realised.

The outlines in 1948 of the warehouses and offices that lined Cannon Street before the Blitz of 29 December 1940. This was the worst air raid of the war on London to that date and although the surrounding streets were devastated, St Paul's, by a miracle, was saved. At the bottom left is Anderson's rubber warehouse and beyond is the square burnt-out tower of St Augustine Watling Street, which has now been restored and incorporated into St Paul's Cathedral Choir School. Reconstruction of this area was not to begin for several years and many bombed sites were used as temporary car parks.

The Central Criminal Court or Old Bailey from the Stone Gallery of St Paul's in 1953. This building which occupies the site of the notorious Newgate Prison was severely damaged during the bombing raids of the war. The nearby St Sepulchre Church dating from the fifteenth century was spared, but the area in the foreground surrounding Paternoster Row was decimated on the night of 29 December 1940. The publishers and booksellers in the street lost six million books during that night. St Paul's was surrounded on three sides by flames but the incendiary bombs that fell on the cathedral were quickly extinguished. The rebuilt Paternoster Square precinct with a sixteen-storey tower was criticised from its inception and has now been demolished to be replaced by low-rise buildings and an attractive square.

The view towards Cheapside from St Paul's, 1953. St Vedast-alias-Foster in the centre was one of many Wren churches which were bomb-damaged – this church was reconstructed in the late 1950s. The church beyond and to the left – St Alban Wood Street – another Wren church, was also gutted. In this instance the shell of the church was demolished in 1955 and the tower restored to be con-verted into a house in 1984–1985. In the left foreground is Nicholson's, one of the few stores left in the vicinity – on its roof a workman is climbing the flagpole to raise a flag in celebration of the Coronation of Queen Elizabeth II.

Above: The Pool of London from the Monument in 1948, with a ship preparing to sail under Tower Bridge. The roof and front of Billingsgate Market is on the immediate right – in the early morning the market and surrounding streets would be full of porters and traders carrying boxes of all varieties of fish. Long considered a nuisance in this position, the market was transferred to the Isle of Dogs in 1982. In the centre foreground is the Coal Exchange, demolished in 1962 for road–widening and beyond, with its long river frontage, is the Custom House. In the left background is the White Tower of the Tower of London.

Left: The view towards the Monument and Tower Bridge from St Paul's in 1953. In the centre is Wren's St Mary Aldermary which fortunately came through the war relatively unscathed and is where Samuel Pepys was married. On the extreme right is the burnt out tower of St Mildred's, the only remaining part of the church where Percy Bysshe Shelley married Mary Wollstonecraft.

St Mary-le-Bow church with its porch and tower standing aside from the gutted nave in 1953. The bells of the church which called Dick Whittington to turn again have been famous since 1091. The present steeple built by Sir Christopher Wren is considered to be his masterpiece and not since the 1960s, when the area surrounding it was rebuilt, has it been possible to appreciate its full glory. The church was restored by Laurence King between 1956 and 1972 by which time new office building had ensured that unrestricted views of the church were a thing of the past.

Opposite: Sunlight streams into Liverpool Street Station in 1946. The station was one of the sights of London, despite having suffered considerable damage during the Blitz. The Gothic tower which surmounted the entrance was destroyed along with much of the building's façade. The station was built by the Great Eastern Railway Co. in 1874 on the site of the Bethlem Royal Hospital, known as Bedlam, and quickly became London's busiest terminal. The forward-looking plans drawn up after the war for modernisation of the station, including a helicopter landing pad on the roof, never materialised. Liverpool Street Station has now been incorporated into the Broadgate complex with an amphitheatre and piazzas.

Right: Traffic crossing Tower Bridge in 1947. The bridge, which from planning to completion took eighteen years, was considered a folly by many, but has since become one of the most popular landmarks of London. There is only a narrow roadway on the bridge; numerous policemen are seen here regulating traffic crossing the river. The Tower Bridge Exhibition, now housed in the towers, takes visitors back to the 1890s to learn the story of the bridge from its conception to the present day.

Left: A Beefeater or Yeoman Warder of the Tower of London in 1947, wearing the long dark blue, undress coat and Tudor bonnet. They are a popular attraction at the Tower and no family album is complete without a photograph of one of the warders. All Yeoman Warders are ex-warrant officers, or their equivalent ranks, and while Warders of the Tower, hold the rank of a regimental sergeant major.

A cargo boat tied up at New Fresh Wharf in 1948. This was still the heyday of the Port of London, despite the considerable damage to the docks and warehouses caused during the Blitz of the Second World War. Many visitors to London were unaware of the scale of the docks which had forty-five miles of quays. Between 1967 and 1981 all the great docks closed, victim of new cargo-handling techniques at the container ports of Tilbury and Felixstowe. The London Docklands Development Corporation was set up to administer the changes as grim warehouses gave way to modern office blocks and apartments. The warehouse in the background here was demolished and replaced by a modern office block.

A small cargo boat sailing under Tower Bridge in 1947. In as little time as a minute the twelve-hundred ton arms of the bridge can be raised to allow a ship through. This happened 655 times in the first month of its operation in 1894 but now the bridge is opened on average only forty times a month. When the bridge was the gateway to London and the Pool was crowded with shipping, a tug was kept riding at anchor, but with steam up, to be of assistance to a ship in difficulties and endangering the bridge.

A tug in the Pool of London in 1949 – one of the hundreds then operating on the River Thames. The warehouses on the far south bank of the Thames have all now been demolished to be replaced by the new Greater London Assembly Building.

The skyline from Waterloo Bridge in 1953, before office blocks and towers rose to compete with St Paul's for dominance. Moored by the Victoria Embankment, from the left are Captain Scott's *Discovery*, HQS *Wellington* and HMS *President* and *Chrysanthemum*. The latter two ships which saw service in the First World War were converted into headquarters and training ships of the Royal Naval Volunteer Reserve. The *Chrysanthemum* has been scrapped but the *President* is now the headquarters of Inter–Action, an educational trust. The wedding cake spire of St Bride's is visible in the centre of the picture – the only part of the church remaining after an air raid in 1940.

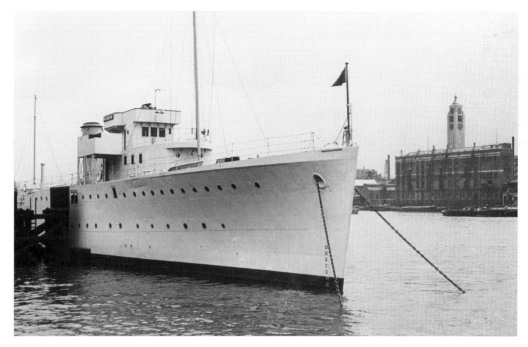

HQS *Wellington*, the Livery Hall of the Honour-able Company of Master Mariners moored by Temple Bar in 1949. The sloop, which was built in Devonport in 1934, served on the New Zealand and China stations before the war, during which she was primarily on convoy escort duties in the North Atlantic. When the *Wellington* was decom-missioned by the Admiralty in 1947, the Company of Master Mariners bought the ship and converted it into a floating Livery Hall. Across the river is the Oxo warehouse, built in 1928, which displays its trademark in all directions. The tower now has a restaurant and viewing platform on the eighth floor giving spectacular views over London.

The *Discovery* moored near Waterloo Bridge in 1949. This was the ship in which Captain R.F. Scott made his first expedition to the Antarctic in 1901. From 1905-1912 the boat was owned by the Hudson Bay Company and during the First World War carried munitions to Russia. In 1929-1931 the *Discovery* made another voyage to the Antarctic with a team of explorers and in 1937 was converted into a training ship for Sea Scouts. After a period as a recruiting headquarters for the Royal Navy, the ship was transferred in 1980 to St Katherine Dock before it sailed to Dundee in 1986 to be opened there as a museum.

Above: Four river boats with army cadets leaving Charing Cross Pier for a cruise in 1946. These boats were part of the thirteen-strong Thames Hospital Emergency Transport Service which was formed at the outbreak of the Second World War. All these cruisers took part in the evacuation of allied troops from Dunkirk in 1940. At the end of the war these boats were bought by Thames Launches and for thirty years were used as pleasure craft. In 1979 the boats were acquired by Tidal Cruisers and modernised with their decks entirely enclosed. The *Marchioness* – the third boat from the left – was sunk on the River Thames in 1989 following a collision with an ocean-going dredger, with the loss of fifty-one lives.

Opposite: The *Odelia,* a river launch, passing St Thomas's Hospital in 1953. The hospital was built in 1868-1971 in the Continental style with pavilions, and approved by Florence Nightingale who established the Nightingale Training School of Nursing here. To this day the nurses at St Thomas's Hospital are known as 'Nightingales'. Of the seven original pavilions facing the river, only the three to the right of the chapel now remain. The four buildings nearest to Westminster Bridge were severely damaged during the war and were replaced by a thirteen-storey hospital block.

Left above: Trams on Victoria Embankment in 1950, two years before the last tram ran in central London. The first electric trams in London were run by Clifton Robinson in 1901, followed in 1903 by the London County Council, but it was not until 1906 that permission was given for trams to run along Victoria Embankment and over Westminster Bridge. In the 1930s the replacement of trams by trolley buses began and this well-loved form of transport began to disappear from the streets of London. Almost half a century later, in 1999, a modern tram system was inaugurated in Croydon.

Left below: People strolling on Waterloo Bridge in 1953. The present bridge replaced John Rennie's bridge of 1817 which was considered a masterpiece. In the 1920s a dangerous settlement in the foundations of the pier arches was discovered and a temporary bridge was built in 1925. After a long controversy the old bridge was demolished and although construction of the new bridge began before the war, it was not completed until 1942. Beyond the bridge is the river frontage of Somerset House, then mainly occupied by government offices and now housing the Courtauld Institute of Art Gallery.

Opposite: The south bank of the River Thames in 1953. The Festival of Britain held in 1951 transformed this previously derelict area into an eye-catching exhibition centre. The Royal Festival Hall on the extreme left was the only building intended to be permanent and the river bank between Waterloo Bridge and Hungerford Railway Bridge was laid out as a promenade. Beyond the railway bridge, which has had a new footbridge built on each side, are the government buildings on Victoria Embankment and the Victorian Gothic Palace of Westminster.

British Railways Standard 4-6-2 Britannia class Pacific No. 70004 *William Shakespeare* locomotive, which headed the Golden Arrow train leaving Victoria Railway Station for Dover in 1953. This locomotive had been on display at the South Bank Exhibition of the Festival of Britain in 1951, before being introduced into service with the Southern Region later that year. Holidays abroad were still a rarity for the average Briton and those who made the crossing to the continent were restricted to a £25 travel allowance. The glamour of this train and the opulence of the first-class compartments was equal to the Orient Express in Europe.

The British Overseas Airways Corporation (BOAC) headquarters on Buckingham Palace Road, 1949. The building was constructed in 1939 for Imperial Airways, the predecessor of BOAC, and has a monumental sculpture above the entrance. With the huge increase in air travel, the original pre-war terminal building has been considerably enlarged.

Holidaymakers waiting at the Victoria Coach Station in 1960. Holidays for most Britons were still taken at a nearby resort – Londoners favouring seaside towns in Essex, Kent and Sussex. Coach travel was then relatively cheap, although slower than rail travel and some patient waiting was usually inevitable.

Left: The sleek de Havilland Comet airliner taking off from Heathrow for Johannesburg in 1953. Flights commenced in May 1952 inaugurating the world's first jet-plane passenger service. Five stops of one hour each were made during the flights which were completed in twenty-three hours. Sadly, this airliner was beset by problems, and in 1954 a Comet crashed into the sea shortly after taking off from Rome with the loss of thirty-five lives. Metal fatigue was judged to be the cause of the crash which effectively ended the airliner's life for commercial transport.

Sappers of the Royal Engineers drained the lake in St James's Park in 1946 to search for an unexploded bomb. It was known to have fallen two hundred yards from the gates of Buckingham Palace in an air raid in 1940 but never located. The crowd, which appears to be highly entertained by the exercise, should surely have been kept further away from such an event! The iron suspension bridge across the lake was replaced by a concrete structure in the 1950s.

One of the finest views in London – the scene from the bridge over the lake in St James's Park, 1953. The crowded domes and spires of Whitehall resemble the Kremlin or an oriental palace when seen here from London's oldest park. There are, in fact, three great buildings in view – Horse Guards, the domed War Office and the roof of the National Liberal Club.

People saunter down Whitehall, passing Downing Street, in 1951. On this Sunday afternoon the street is quiet with few tourists and little traffic. Building work was due to begin here at this time across Whitehall on the site of Montague House, the London home of the Duke of Buccleuch. Latterly, the house had been occupied by the Ministry of Labour and new government buildings were due to take its place.

The Clock Tower of the Houses of Parliament, known as Big Ben, certainly the best-known sight of London. The perfectly-proportioned tower balances the taller Victoria Tower to the south. Parliament Square is still an oasis surrounded by rushing traffic with many statues of great statesmen on the lawns.

The statue of Boadicea driving her war chariot (without reins) to victory over the Romans, accompanied by her two daughters. The statuary group was erected to commemorate the Queen of the Iceni who burnt the Roman colonies of Colchester, St Albans and London in AD 60. In the background is Big Ben in which a lamp is lit at night to indicate that Parliament is sitting.

The Houses of Parliament and its parish church, St Margaret's, in 1953. The church is dwarfed by its neighbour – Westminster Abbey – but is a welcome sanctuary from the constant traffic in Victoria Street. Monks from the abbey founded St Margaret's in the eleventh century with a similar motive – to escape from the bustle of the cathedral to a refuge of peace.

Opposite: French Canadians take over guard duty from the Welsh Guards at Buckingham Palace in 1945. Orders in French and English were read by the French Canadian corporal on the right. During the Second World War soldiers from many Commonwealth countries undertook guard duties at the palace, invariably attracting a crowd of spectators.

Above: A sergeant of the Scots Guards, checking the new guard at Buckingham Palace in 1948. Three years after the end of the Second World War, full-dress ceremonial uniform was still not worn by the troops guarding the palace. Sentry boxes were provided for use on rainy days.

An immaculate and resplendent Grenadier Guard on duty outside Buckingham Palace in 1953. By the year of the Coronation, full-dress uniform was worn on ceremonial occasions. The sentries were then positioned outside the palace railings having no need of protection from the public.

LONDON – LIFE IN THE POST-WAR YEARS

Tourists on the steps of the Queen Victoria Memorial watch the Changing of the Guard in 1948. The Americans in the centre – the man with a Paillard Bolex ciné-camera – were among many visitors from the United States who were arriving in greater numbers. Their affluence was in sharp contrast to that of the British who were still restricted and rationed. The Americans were welcome both for themselves and also for their dollars which were vital to Britain's economy at a time when its balance of payments situation was precarious.

35

The Life Guards of the Corps of the Household Cavalry in the Mall in 1948. This, the senior regiment of the British Army, having been founded in 1659 to promote the Cavalier cause, was still at this time performing ceremonial duties in khaki uniform.

The Royal Horse Guards (The Blues), clattering through Hyde Park on their way to Horse Guards in 1949. This is one of the great moments of a London morning when the troop of Horse Guards in their full regalia ride down to Whitehall to perform their guard duties. The Royal Horse Guards were raised by Charles II in 1661 and are distinguished from the Life Guards by their red plumes and blue uniforms.

Opposite: A Life Guard on duty at Horse Guards, 1953. The two sentries in Whitehall are so much a part of the capital's pageantry that many visitors feel they have not really seen London until they have stood in awe before them.

A Royal Horse Guard on sentry duty in Whitehall in 1949. Standing motionless, with the peaks of their brass helmets almost on the bridge of their noses and with their huge spurred boots, the guards are regarded with affection by Londoners and tourists alike.

The rehearsal of the Trooping the Colour in 1948 which never took place. These are the Coldstream Guards who were to troop their colour on the official birthday of King George VI. Rain was forecast on the morning of the event and the ceremony was cancelled, but ironically the weather at Horse Guards Parade was perfect at the time fixed for the parade. This was to have been the first occasion since 1939 that the Brigade of Guards were in full ceremonial uniform for the trooping. The great crowd which had assembled were eventually informed of the cancellation by an officer of the Guards who announced, 'We cannot afford to have the full-dress tunics spoilt when they are no longer our property but public property. No more uniforms can be made and there is only a limited number available'.

A Coldstream Guard on duty at the rehearsal of the Trooping the Colour that never was in 1948. An MP subsequently writing to *The Times* maintained, 'The crowds were willing to chance a thunderstorm and the troops could presumably have braved the same perils as the public'. Another writer suggested the War Office should find an old farmer, preferably with rheumatism, to stand on the roof of Horse Guards to give an accurate local weather forecast. On only one other occasion since the war has the Trooping the Colour ceremony been cancelled, when in 1955 a rail strike caused the event to be abandoned. More recently, in 2001, the ceremony continued despite appalling conditions when a cloud burst turned Horse Guards parade into a lake and the participants and crowd were drenched.

Opposite: Piccadilly viewed from Green Park, 1950. This stretch of Piccadilly was known as Rothschild Row due to several members of the banking family who lived here in the early 1900s. The most famous of these houses was 145 Piccadilly, the home of the Duke and Duchess of York in 1936 when the Duke succeeded to the throne following the abdication of King Edward VIII. The house, which had been severely damaged during the war, was demolished when Hyde Park Corner was redeveloped in 1959 and the remainder of these houses were swept away in the 1970s when the Inn on the Park and the Intercontinental Hotels were built.

Right: The Duke of Windsor emerging from Lock's the hatters in St James's Street, 1945. After the Duke resigned as Governor of the Bahamas in March 1945 he and the Duchess of Windsor spent some time in America and France before he returned alone to Britain in October 1945, staying with his mother, Queen Mary, at Marlborough House. During his three-month stay in Britain, the Duke carried out tours of the bombed areas in the East End of London, paid several visits to King George VI and met politicians. Lock & Company was founded in 1676 when Robert Davis opened a hatter's shop at the south-east end of St James's Street. James Lock inherited the business in 1759 and the family connection has continued to the present day. Among the many famous men who have had headgear supplied by Lock's are Lord Nelson and the Duke of Wellington.

The Park Lane Hotel on Piccadilly in 1950. The hotel was so named from its close proximity to the old Park Lane although during its lengthy construction in the 1920s due to lack of money, it was nicknamed the Birdcage. When completed, this was the most up-to-date hotel in London and its Art Deco ballroom was considered the finest in the capital. Parts of the hotel were used as locations for the Atlantic liner scenes in the BBC television production of *Brideshead Revisited*. In the centre of the photograph is a pre-war Morris Super-Six 14-horsepower taxicab and above are two men in a cradle cleaning the windows of the hotel.

Road menders at Hyde Park Corner in 1950. Workmen are asphalting the road surface with hot tar and stone chippings. In those days this task was performed manually, the tar being carried from the flaming cauldron in wheelbarrows and spread evenly over the road.

Traffic on the ring road of Hyde Park near Stanhope Gate in 1949, heavy then as now, with a policeman on the road attempting to calm the flow of cars. The Dorchester Hotel is in the left background and to the right are several Victorian mansions most of which have now been demolished. Inside the railings to the right is the Cavalry War Memorial by Adrian Jones, removed to Serpentine Road in Hyde Park in 1961 when Park Lane was made into a dual carriageway.

Sunlight glints on the spray of the Joy of Life fountain near Broad Walk in Hyde Park in 1963. The fountain, which was designed by T.B. Huxley-Jones, was given by the Constance Fund, an organisation founded in 1944 by Mrs C. Goetze in memory of her husband. Hyde Park was opened to the public in 1637 and since then has been used for a variety of activities including military manoeuvres, concerts, exhibitions, relaxing and boating on the lake. During the Second World War sheep grazed in the park and gun emplacements and barrage balloons were sited there.

The Dorchester Hotel, Park Lane in 1948, an institution since it opened in 1931. The hotel was built on the site of Dorchester House, later Hertford House which was modelled on the Villa Farnese in Rome. During the war the Dorchester was the headquarters of General Eisenhower, and with its reinforced concrete structure was considered one of the safest buildings in London. Since the war, the hotel has had many famous guests including Charlton Heston, Judy Garland, Walt Disney and Noel Coward but the Dorchester's most faithful star visitor was Elizabeth Taylor.

The London Hilton Hotel, Park Lane in 1963 – the year it was opened. Accused at the time of violating the London skyline, criticism has diminished since the construction of other tower blocks around Hyde Park. The roof-top bar and restaurant offer spectacular views over the whole of central London. The hotel, which was built by Charles Clore on the site of a row of bomb-damaged Regency houses, rapidly became popular with the new international jet-setters.

Regency houses on Park Lane in 1953. These houses, dating from the early nineteenth century, originally had entrances to the east and these bow windows faced their gardens and Hyde Park. With the creation of Park Lane, the gardens disappeared and these houses with their expanse of glass were left in close proximity to the traffic. The first house in the row, at the corner of Pitt's Head Mews, which commemorates William Pitt the Elder, has recently been demolished to be replaced by offices and residential apartments. The smaller adjoining house with its angular bow front has been spared but is now sandwiched between modern buildings.

The statue of President Roosevelt in Grosvenor Square in 1949. Planned during the war, the statue, designed by Sir William Reid Dick, was unveiled by Mrs Eleanor Roosevelt in 1948. The cost of the statue was met within a week by donations (of not more than 5s each) from the British public. The square, the largest in Mayfair, no longer has iron railings and is more informal. The buildings in the square have been mainly reconstructed and given over to embassies, hotels and apartments.

The American Embassy in Grosvenor Square, 1949. This was built in 1937 but in the 1950s a massive new embassy with a 999-year lease was constructed on the west side of the square, which had been heavily bombed during the war. Throughout the conflict the lovely garden in the centre of the square was turned to practical use when a crew of the Women's Auxiliary Air Force manned a barrage balloon here – they named it Romeo! The cars in front of the embassy are both American, a Cadillac on the left and a Packard on the right.

Two smartly uniformed sergeants of the US Marines at ease in Grosvenor Square in 1949. The United States Marine Corps, which was founded in 1775 as an arm of the US Navy, man the American embassies throughout the world. In the background are buildings damaged during the war and still awaiting reconstruction.

Left above: An American Oldsmobile with gleaming chrome in Grosvenor Square, 1948. In the background are the offices of Way & Waller, one of London's pre-eminent estate agents. The early period after the war was a time when many great houses of Mayfair were empty, either through bomb damage or because their owners now found them too expensive to run. Many were sold and replaced by modern buildings.

Left below: The Cumberland Hotel at Marble Arch in 1949. The Cumberland, which was opened in 1933, was the first hotel in London with a thousand rooms, each with an adjoining bathroom. The hotel was built to attract American tourists and businessmen and from its opening was equipped with soda fountains and air-conditioning. The rooms were all fitted to a high standard and were then 22s for a single and 36s 6d for a double room. The Marble Arch on the left was originally erected in front of Buckingham Palace but was transferred to its present site for the Great Exhibition of 1851 and stood as the original entrance to Hyde Park.

Opposite: Relaxing in Hyde Park in 1952. Hyde Park has been a place of relaxation and fashion since the sixteenth century and together with the adjoining Kensington Gardens forms the largest park in central London.

An orator at Speakers' Corner, near Marble Arch, 1949. The speaker seems determined to read from his sermons although the attention of his audience appears to be elsewhere. The right to hold assemblies here was granted in 1872 after a series of angry demonstrations, but police retain full jurisdiction over the speakers.

A speaker at Marble Arch in 1949 who appears to be deriving some amusement from his audience. Orators at this famous spot include extremists, eccentrics and the most earnest of religious speakers, each with a circle of listeners.

A button-holed speaker in Hyde Park with oversized pages of religious tracts in 1949. This well-dressed man in pin-striped trousers is well prepared with a ladder giving him an advantage over his audience. Most speakers seem to enjoy the cut-and-thrust of the exchanges even though the listeners may be unconvinced by the orators' messages.

An audience at Speakers' Corner in 1949. On Sundays this part of Hyde Park still attracts many people to hear the assortment of orators holding forth. In the 1940s men invariably wore a jacket and tie, whatever they were doing and wherever they were going.

Opposite: Oxford Street from the Cumberland Hotel in 1950. Shoppers and strollers cross the sunny road, half of which is being resurfaced. The east-bound traffic has been re-routed adding to the road problems of this part of London. A barrow boy has taken advantage of the partial road closure to site his stall on the roadway. The south and shady side of Oxford Street never possessed any great department stores but the north side boasted Selfridges, John Lewis, Marshall & Snelgrove, Bourne & Hollingsworth and D.H. Evans.

Right above: The Cumberland Hotel, Marble Arch, 1949. The hotel and adjoining Lyons Corner House attracted many tourists and businessmen. The Cumberland has eight floors below ground level – these were invaluable during the war when they were used as air–raid shelters. In the foreground is a 12-horsepower Austin low-loader taxicab, already superseded by the Austin FX3, introduced in 1948 and destined to become London's 'Black cab'.

Right below: The Odeon Cinema at Marble Arch in 1948. The Odeon chain was founded by Oscar Deutsch who opened his first cinema at Perry Bar, Birmingham, in 1930. With cinema-going at its peak, Odeon theatres were opened throughout the country and by 1944 there were 318 cinemas in the group. This building, completed in 1933, was intended to complement the Cumberland Hotel across Cumberland Place and set off the nearby Marble Arch.

This page:
Above: Shop-window gazers at Dolcis shoe shop on Oxford Street in 1949.

Below: A spectacular array of hats in C&A Modes shop window on Oxford Street in 1949. This vast store, then one of the major attractions for shoppers at Marble Arch, had numerous floors and departments. These stylish hats, copies of the latest Parisian models perhaps, ranged in price from 7s 6d to 35s 6d.

Opposite page:
Left: The return of London's lights in 1945. The blackout of windows ended on 23 April, but so many homes switched on their lights in celebration that they caused power failures. Street lighting remained switched off until 25 July to give electricians time to restore the lamps. These American soldiers, and a girlfriend, admire the lights near City Road.

Right above: Broadcasting House in Portland Place, 1949. The headquarters of the BBC opened in 1932 and all the radio programmes, so vital to the morale of the public during the war, were made here. After the end of hostilities, the popularity of radio continued with three distinct programmes being provided – the middle-brow *Home Service*, the popular *Light Programme* and the highbrow *Third Programme*.

Right below: The newly neon-lit shopfront of His Master's Voice in Oxford Street in 1949. Television sets were on sale here but programmes were only broadcast for a few hours a day to the London area and audiences were minimal. Record players were popular but the 78 rpm, shellac discs of the period were highly breakable and only played for three or four minutes on each side.

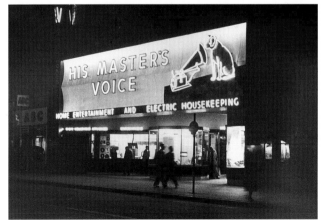

Piccadilly Circus in 1948, sparsely decorated for the Olympic Games of that year. Pennants hang from poles on each side of Shaftesbury Avenue and Boots the Chemists have hung a Union Jack outside their shop. There appears to be no traffic control and pedestrians cross the road at all points. The globes on the lamp standards, which were removed during the war, have been replaced but the illuminated advertisements were still not to be lit for another year.

Piccadilly Circus in 1948. The London Pavilion, with its two façades covered in advertisements, is showing Dick Powell in *To the Ends of the Earth*. A hoarding in Coventry Street advertises the Andrews Sisters at the London Palladium – Hollywood stars who appeared there included Carmen Miranda, Danny Kaye, Bob Hope and Perry Como. Dodging the traffic are two men in dark suits, each with an umbrella and both wearing hats – the uniform of the period.

Illuminated signs in Piccadilly Circus, 1949. Regulations which prohibited illuminated advertisements ended on 3 April 1949 and crowds flocked to Piccadilly Circus to watch the lights being switched on again. Four years after the end of the Second World War, the public were still suffering from restrictions – clothes rationing had only just ended, but rationing of petrol was not to end until 1950.

A stylish New Look dress attracts attention to a display in Swan & Edgar's shop window in Piccadilly Circus, in 1949. The style is in sharp contrast to the dress of some of the onlookers! After the long war years of 'making do', many of the new and more elegant post-war fashions were quickly copied by a nation of home dressmakers.

Opposite: Piccadilly Circus in 1952. The Bovril sign was one of the first illuminated advertisements to appear here in 1910 and others including the Guinness clock became equally famous although *The Times* in 1928 described the lights as 'a hideous eyesore which no civilised community ought to tolerate'. Since 1977 the façade of the London Pavilion has been cleared of all neon signs, revealing its elegant exterior.

The splendid sweep of the Quadrant, the alternative name of this stretch of Regent Street from Piccadilly Circus in 1950. After a century of service, John Nash's elegant buildings were demolished in 1924 and Sir Reginald Blomfield designed this new shopping street.

Among the restaurants along this part of Regent Street are the Café Royal – a well-known bohemian haunt – and Veeraswamy, an Indian restaurant famous since the 1920s.

American tourists are among the pedestrians crossing Shaftesbury Avenue in 1953. London in the weeks preceding the Coronation of Queen Elizabeth II was crowded with visitors, particularly from America, and hotel rooms were at a premium. Frank's Barber Shop on the left had been a well-known feature of Piccadilly Circus since 1911.

Shaftesbury Avenue, 1959. The street was built in 1886 as part of a slum clearance programme and quickly became London's leading entertainment district with six theatres between Piccadilly Circus and Cambridge Circus. The London Pavilion on the right which was opened as a theatre in 1885, and later converted into a cinema, has now become Rock Circus, a museum of rock and pop music. Beyond is the Trocadero Restaurant built in 1896 with its famous Long Bar, and advertised at the time as the 'premier restaurant in the world' – it has now been transformed into an entertainment centre.

Piccadilly Circus in 1953. This awkwardly-shaped junction at the heart of London's West End was, after the war, the subject of several redevelopment proposals. Most involved demolishing the north-east section of the Circus, replacing it with tower blocks but fortunately none of them were implemented. The Circus may not be the most beautiful sight in London but it remains a popular venue for millions of tourists each year.

A news vendor selling the *Evening News* in Piccadilly,1953. There were then three evening papers published in London – the *Evening News*, associated with the *Daily Mail*, the *Evening Standard* from Lord Beaverbrook's Express group and the *Star* published by the *News Chronicle*. Invariably these would be sold by news vendors standing only yards apart although some newspaper sellers would handle all three titles and their cry of 'News, Star, Standard!', was quite familiar.

Piccadilly Circus in 1949 with the plinth of the Statue of Eros providing convenient seating for visitors and American servicemen. Women flower sellers were then a regular feature of the roundabout – with their shawls, feathered bonnets and voluminous skirts, they were world-famous and Piccadilly Circus is not the same without them.

The Statue of Eros in a decorative cage for the Coronation in 1953. Nowadays the statue is regularly boarded up on New Year's Eve and on other occasions when large crowds are expected. Swan & Edgar's department store and the County Fire Office in the centre were the only buildings completed when a plan for the rebuilding of Piccadilly Circus was proposed in the early twentieth century.

Three visitors from the provinces pose for the camera in Piccadilly Circus in 1953. Throughout the summer, thousands of people traced the route taken by Queen Elizabeth II after her Coronation.

The Warner Cinema, Cranbourn Street, in 1949, built in 1937 on the site of Daly's Theatre. Cinemas and shops were at last permitted to use illuminated signs and the streets between Leicester Square and Piccadilly Circus were ablaze with lights. This was the age of mass cinema-going and the first-run cinemas of the West End attracted big audiences to see the latest films. After being premièred in the West End, new films were shown for a week in cinemas in the north-west of London, followed by a week in the north-east and then shown south of the Thames.

The Empire Cinema in Leicester Square in 1949, built in 1928 on the site of the Empire Theatre. Most films shown in British cinemas were made in Hollywood but the Rank Organisation and Ealing Studios produced distinctive and popular films such as *Maytime in Mayfair*, being shown here, starring Anna Neagle and Michael Wilding.

Opposite: Coventry Street in the rain, 1953. The Mapleton Hotel in common with most London hotels in Coronation year was having to refuse bookings. A suite of rooms here cost 35s a night, the sitting room having a bed which folded up to the wall. The taxi on the left is a 14-horsepower Beardmore Paramount model introduced in 1933 which, along with Austin and Morris cabs, were the mainstay of taxi operators before the war.

Coventry Street from the Mapleton Hotel in 1948. The building opposite appears unscathed by the war but the Café de Paris, which was in the basement of the block, received a direct hit in an air raid in 1941. The night club was advertised as 'the safest place to dance in town', being twenty feet beneath the Rialto Cinema, but a bomb fell through an air shaft killing eighty-four of the diners and dancers. It was left derelict for two years then the club was reopened as a dance hall for troops, with an entrance fee of 6d. After the war, the Café de Paris reopened, regaining some of its old magic with its tea dances, but closed in 1957. In 1996 it reopened again as a night club and restaurant.

Coventry Street in 1948. The Victorian Queens House on the right is a bar and the Monseigneur News Theatre is showing the latest newsreels of the Olympic Games then being held in the capital. The adjoining Empire Cinema is presenting Judy Garland and Gene Kelly in *The Pirate*. The taxicab on the right is a 12-horsepower Austin low-loader – of the 6,700 cabs running in London before the war, less than 3,000 survived. On the extreme left is a Post Office telegraph boy with his pouch attached to his belt and his hat in his hand.

Visitors relax in Leicester Square, away from the crowded streets of the West End, a few days before the Coronation of Queen Elizabeth II in 1953. The Empire Cinema, with its panoramic screen is topically showing *Young Bess* starring Jean Simmons, Stewart Granger, Deborah Kerr and Charles Laughton. The Monseigneur News Theatre programme typically lasted an hour and included two newsreels, cartoons and a short topical film.

The Odeon Cinema in Leicester Square, 1948, showing Lawrence Olivier's *Hamlet*. The black granite cinema, the flagship of the Odeon chain, was built in 1937 on the site of the Alhambra Theatre. The cinema opened with a royal charity performance of *The Prisoner of Zenda* starring Ronald Colman, since which time there have been countless film premières. The cinema still has a single screen auditorium, capable of holding almost 2,000 people and recently a VIP glass balcony facing the square has been built. On the left is the recently rebuilt Café Anglais, destroyed by a direct hit in a wartime raid.

Left above: The National Gallery and St Martin-in-the-Fields in 1953. On the left, in front of the National Gallery, scaffolding is being erected to hold the viewing stands being built on the processional route of the forthcoming Coronation. This section of road is now closed to traffic and pedestrians can walk from the National Gallery to the square without hazard.

Left below: Trafalgar Square in 1949. The southern side of the square consists mainly of rather dull Victorian commercial buildings, although the view down Whitehall is more impressive. This large open space in the centre of tourist London is where most visitors congregate to rest and plan their next move. The granite fountains and basins were completed in 1845 and remodelled in 1939 by Sir Edwin Lutyens as a memorial to Earl Beatty and Earl Jellicoe.

Opposite: The Theatre Royal Haymarket, also known as the Haymarket Theatre, in 1964. The theatre, the second on the site, was built in 1821 by John Nash as part of his design for a grand thoroughfare between the Prince Regent's palace, Carlton House and Marylebone Park, now Regent's Park. This theatre is one of the few survivors of that plan and is almost unique in having a rear elevation as interesting as the front. Sir Ralph Richardson was appearing in Graham Greene's *Carving a Statue* with Roland Culver, Dennis Waterman and Jane Birkin.

Opposite: Floodlit fountains in Trafalgar Square, 1953. The mermen, mermaids and dolphins sculpted in bronze and spouting water, were added to the Lutyens' fountains after the Second World War.

Above: A sunny afternoon in Trafalgar Square in 1953. The glorious church of St Martin-in-the-Fields, the model for many other churches especially in America, has a long tradition of caring for the homeless and unfortunate. For years now, Trafalgar Square has been the traditional site of social and political meetings. In 1996 Nelson Mandela addressed thousands of people from the balcony of South Africa House, just to the right of the photograph.

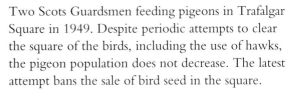

Two Scots Guardsmen feeding pigeons in Trafalgar Square in 1949. Despite periodic attempts to clear the square of the birds, including the use of hawks, the pigeon population does not decrease. The latest attempt bans the sale of bird seed in the square.

A young boy with a pigeon in Trafalgar Square in 1945. Perhaps tired of wheeling around the square, the bird seems to be giving the boy a lesson in cooing.

The Aldwych in 1949. This is a twentieth-century crescent, but the architecture is reminiscent of the nineteenth century. There are two theatres here, the Strand and the Aldwych and the massive Waldorf Hotel which later became the Strand Palace Hotel and is now offices. The small Evening News van in vivid yellow is in contrast to the London bus in red.

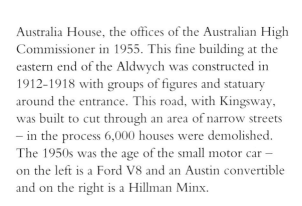

Australia House, the offices of the Australian High Commissioner in 1955. This fine building at the eastern end of the Aldwych was constructed in 1912-1918 with groups of figures and statuary around the entrance. This road, with Kingsway, was built to cut through an area of narrow streets – in the process 6,000 houses were demolished. The 1950s was the age of the small motor car – on the left is a Ford V8 and an Austin convertible and on the right is a Hillman Minx.

The *Lancet* offices in Adam Street in 1953. This elegant building is one of the few to remain from the Adelphi, an eighteenth–century project of the Adam brothers. They planned to build a series of streets of houses in one consistent pattern but the scheme was never completed. In the 1930s many Adam houses were demolished to make way for modern office blocks. Adam House, as it is now called, with its impressive façade and equally fine interior is now a suite of offices. The house on the left was, in the eighteenth century, occupied by Sir Richard Arkwright, the inventor and mill owner.

The Strand in the rain in 1948 from the entrance of Moon's Garage.
Across the street, as busy then as it is today, are Mooney's Irish Bar,
Slaters restaurant and Marjorie Moores Marriage Bureau, this being
one of few such agencies in London at the time. The Strand, famous
for the Savoy Hotel and Simpson's Restaurant was also a street of
specialist shops and businesses, including stamp dealers.

Left: Women sitting in Lincoln's Inn Fields in 1953, enjoying a gossip. This is one of the largest squares in London and is very peaceful, with the bustle of the traffic kept at bay.

Opposite: Two of London's landmarks – the Savoy Hotel and Shell-Mex House overlooking the Thames. The Savoy was the brainchild of Richard D'Oyly Carte the impressario and when it opened in 1889 incorporated previously unheard of features, including full electric lighting and what for the time, was a startling number of baths – sixty-seven in total. The celebrated hotelier Cesar Ritz was lured from Paris to be the hotel's first manager accompanied by Auguste Escoffier, the famous chef. Many great figures stayed at the Savoy including Sarah Bernhardt, Lily Langtry, Dame Nellie Melba and Enrico Caruso. Among the great events at the hotel was the occasion in 1948 when Mrs Eleanor Roosevelt was the guest of honour of the Pilgrim Society and among the thousand guests was Sir Winston Churchill and the newly married Princess Elizabeth and the Duke of Edinburgh. The Shell-Mex building was built on the site of the famous Cecil Hotel and its Art Deco tower contains the largest public clock in London.

Above: A highly polished French Delage motor car parked on a bomb site near the Strand in 1949. Louis Delage made superb touring cars and his company had many years of success in Grand Prix racing. This Delage is a 1937 D8-120 4.3 litre Deltasport Drophead Foursome Coupé. For many years after the war, bomb sites became oases for wild flowers, as well as providing useful car parks.

Left: The Royal Opera House, Covent Garden, 1959. Behind the impressive portico and the ornate auditorium the Royal Opera and the Royal Ballet shared cramped backstage facilities until the extensive redevelopments of recent years. The 1950s was the decade when the Bolshoi and Kirov ballet companies made their first celebrated appearances here. Car parking was restricted outside the opera house but cars were apparently allowed to park across the street outside Bow Street Magistrates' Court.

Dolores Gray and Neville Mapp with the cast
of *Annie Get Your Gun* at the Coliseum in 1948.
This show, with *Oklahoma!* which was running at
the Theatre Royal, Drury Lane at the same time,
brought in a new style of musical in which songs
were integrated into the plot. *Annie Get Your Gun*
ran for 1,147 performances at the Imperial Theatre
in New York and the London production ran for
four years at the Coliseum.

Sir Charles B. Cochran with the cast of *Bless the
Bride* on its last night at the Adelphi Theatre in
1949. C.B. Cochran was famous for his musicals
in the 1920s and 1930s, most of them featuring
his glamorous 'young ladies'. The cast of *Bless the
Bride*, written by A.P. Herbert and Vivian Ellis,
included Edmund Goffron, Lizbeth Webb and
Anona Winn.

Derby County supporters in front of Buckingham Palace in 1946. The fans, with their rosettes and rattles, took in the sights of London before making their way to Wembley Stadium for the cup final against Charlton Athletic. The Derby fans went home happy with their team winning 4–1 after extra time.

A motorcycle speedway meeting at Harringay in 1948. Speedway was very popular in the early post-war years and attendances were high. Harringay raced against Wembley at this meeting and the Harringay captain Vic Duggan, an Australian, and his opposite number Bill Kitchen, were well known for their friendly but competitive rivalry.

Young people on the Waltzer at Blackheath Fair in 1964. Blackheath is ringed by fine houses and has been famous for its fairs since the seventeenth century.

Derby Day at Epsom in 1949. The downs are crowded with spectators who have arrived in buses, cars and trains. Some have brought boxes on which to stand, others are sitting on the roofs of coaches, enjoying a day out in glorious weather. Bookmakers line the racecourse and there are many amusements and refreshment stalls. During the races the noise is deafening. Nimbus won this Derby in a thrilling finish.

The Olympic Games at Wembley Stadium, 1948. These were called the austerity Olympics as no new stadiums were built for the events and there was little ostentation. London was awarded the games with little opposition but British athletes were not very successful, winning no gold medals. The athletic events at Wembley were very well attended – this race was a 400 metres heat won by the Jamaican Arthur Wint who went on to win the final. These games were the first to be televised although coverage was only in the London area and very few television receivers were then in use.

Children queueing for rides on a young elephant at London Zoo in 1950. Brumas, a young polar bear was the star attraction of the year – over three million people visited the zoo to see him.

A street trader in full flow at Petticoat Lane market, 1949. The street, which was renamed Middlesex Street in the nineteenth century, besides being a market where clothes can be bought, has all manner of bric-a-brac for sale. In the years immediately after the war, when goods were in short supply, this market served a useful purpose.

Rass Prince Monolulu sells horse-racing tips to onlookers in Petticoat Lane in 1949. The 'Prince' was a familiar figure at racecourses and elsewhere before and after the war, in full warrior dress with huge multi-coloured ostrich feathers on his head. He sold his race selections at a nominal 6d or 1s each, and although the horse may not have won, it was worth the money merely to talk to him. His cry, 'I've got a horse', became famous, but this giant of a man could draw a crowd by his appearance alone.

Above left: A stallholder in Petticoat Lane in 1950 with a wide range of fancy goods to sell – everything from chromeware to canteens of cutlery, handbags and pearl necklaces. Just like today many of these onlookers will have come to enjoy the entertainment as much as to look for a bargain.

Above right: A couple listening to a salesman in Petticoat Lane in 1949.

Right: A persuasive salesman in Petticoat Lane in 1950. Stallholders often show a ready wit but will also take advantage of customers searching for a bargain. The modern market has now spread into the surrounding streets, each with its own character.

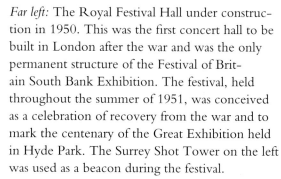

Far left: The Royal Festival Hall under construction in 1950. This was the first concert hall to be built in London after the war and was the only permanent structure of the Festival of Britain South Bank Exhibition. The festival, held throughout the summer of 1951, was conceived as a celebration of recovery from the war and to mark the centenary of the Great Exhibition held in Hyde Park. The Surrey Shot Tower on the left was used as a beacon during the festival.

Left: The South Bank Exhibition from Waterloo Bridge in 1951. The 300ft high Skylon in the centre appeared to hang unsuspended in the air and at night-time was illuminated from within. Although the summer of 1951 was plagued by rain, the festival was a success with crowds flocking to this exhibition and the many others held throughout the country.

The Royal Festival Hall and the Shot Tower from Victoria Embankment in 1951. The South Bank Exhibition was created on a twenty-seven acre site, derelict since the end of the war, and was the beginning of the development of an arts centre on the south side of the Thames. The Shot Tower as well as being open to the public carried scientific apparatus to record radio signals from space.

The Dome of Discovery at the South Bank Exhibition, 1951. The dome, supported on slender struts was, with a 365ft diameter, the largest then constructed. The theme of the exhibits in the dome was British achievements in discovery and exploration – the dominant feature was a huge 74-in telescope made for the Mount Stromlo Observatory in Australia.

A locomotive built for the Indian Government Railway, on display at the Transport Pavilion on the South Bank in 1951. The locomotive is a 2-8-2 W.G. Class No. 8350, one of a hundred built in Glasgow by the North British Locomotive Company. Thereafter they were produced in the Indian Government Railway's own plant at Chitteranjan. Many of these locomotives are still in use in the subcontinent.

The view towards the Houses of Parliament from the South Bank site, 1951. In the foreground are the pylons supporting the Skylon and to the left is the Sea and Ships Pavilion. Over eight million people visited the exhibition during the summer.

The Festival of Britain Exhibition from Westminster Bridge, 1951. The festival was a tonic to the nation after the long years of war and the years of austerity that had followed it. The South Bank Exhibition was not only a trade fair but an informative and enjoyable day out for the family. On the right is County Hall, then the headquarters of the London County Council, but now the home of the Sea Life London Aquarium, the London Film Museum, restaurants and a health club. The site of the Dome of Discovery, which became the Jubilee Gardens in 1977, is now occupied by the London Eye, the 500ft observation wheel built for the Millennium celebrations.

Right above: The Grand Vista at the Festival Pleasure Gardens at Battersea in 1951. This was the lighter side of the Festival of Britain promising entertainment and relaxation for everyone. Within the gardens were open-air cafés, an amusement park, a children's zoo, illuminations and fireworks. Some of the features in the gardens remained after the festival year and a major restoration project is currently under way.

Right below: Neptune, a Rowland Emett-designed locomotive at the Festival Pleasure Gardens, 1951. The architecture in the gardens was intentionally quirky but this miniature railway, the Oyster Creek and Far Tottering Line, with its three outrageous locomotives – the other two were named *Nellie* and *Wild Goose* – was the most absurd. This locomotive has a copper kettle for a funnel and is fitted with a diving helmet, a ship's wheel and horn and a gyroscope.

Overleaf: All the traffic and visitors headed for the Mall in the Coronation year of 1953. This graceful arch – one of four – spanned the processional way leading to Buckingham Palace. The arches, surmounted by two golden lions and two white unicorns, supported a Princess's coronet and were floodlit at night. Stands for spectators lined the whole of the Mall and in front of the palace – these were fully occupied hours before the Coronation procession was due. Cars in the Mall here include a Ford V8 Pilot on the right, behind which is a Standard Vanguard and retreating on the left is a Ford 8, sporting a rear luggage rack.

Flags and bunting for the Coronation of Queen Elizabeth almost obliterate the façades of the newspaper offices in Fleet Street in 1953. The City's flag emblazoned with the blunt sword of St Paul indicates the location. Although this street was not on the processional route, all businesses vied with each other to present the best display.

The newspapers were also competing to give the best coverage of all the events of the summer. *The Times*, which had its own correspondent on the Mount Everest Expedition, was the first newspaper to publish news on Coronation Day of its successful conquest.

Old Bond Street splendidly decorated for the Coronation in 1953. Most streets in the West End were garlanded. On the right is Scott's the hatters, with the Royal coat of arms above the doorway. Scott's was founded in the 1870s taking over from an outfitters which had been in existence since 1758. This was one of the few businesses in London still delivering goods by horse and carriage, with the driver and his companion both dressed in a uniform and top hat. In the early 1970s Scott's amalgamated with Lock's of St James's Street and this shop was then closed.

Right: The tower of Big Ben and a row of banners emblazoned with lions rampant, topped with coronets in 1953.

Far right: The west front of Westminster Abbey in July 1953. As part of the decorations for the entrance to the abbey, James Woodford designed this annexe and also ten Queen's beasts based on royal heraldic animals and cast them as 6ft high figures. After the Coronation, stone replicas of the plaster originals were erected in the Royal Botanic Gardens at Kew.

Below right: London in 1953 saw its biggest ever traffic jams. Throughout the summer, cars, buses and coaches carried neck-craning visitors along the Coronation route. Oxford Street, particularly drew huge crowds of people bringing traffic to a standstill. Selfridge's store, in the background here, was famous for its window displays above which were paintings of famous British characters of the past.

Below: The Dorchester Hotel decorated for the Coronation in 1953. Oliver Messel hung superb decorations on the building both inside and out, and the ballroom was used to serve meals all day just as it had been for King George VI's Coronation in 1937.

The Post Office Tower, now known as the Telecom Tower, from Charlotte Street in 1964. The tower, 580ft in height, was erected to provide un-impeded telecommunications throughout the capital. After a bomb incident in 1971 the viewing platform at the top of the tower was closed but the famous revolving restaurant remained open until 1980.